THE VENTURE CONTINUES
THROUGH PARADISE

MARVIN CRUTCHFIELD

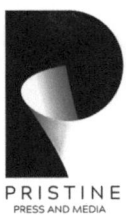
PRISTINE
PRESS AND MEDIA

ISBN
978-1-964804-31-6 (Paperback)
978-1-964804-30-9 (eBook)
978-1-964804-32-3 (Hardcover)

ACKNOWLEDGEMENTS

First and foremost I want to thank Yah the Creator of the earth and also His son Yahuah His Son who was murdered on a tree for me .

Plus the Ruach aka the Holy Spirit

To my parents Harvey and Anna Mae Crutchfield. I wanna thank y'all for the sacrifices y'all made for us. I miss both of y'all terribly. Dad passed away in 1982 and moms passed away in 1983. I was a teen when it happened, but I remembered what I was taught.

To my siblings Harvetta, Pam, Troy and Rose. I hope we never lose our closeness that we had as children growing up. Now to the rest of my family I love all of y'all but it's too many in number to mention. But I always say F.A.M.I.L.Y means family always means I love you.

To my spiritual family my Israelites brothers and sisters. I thank y'all for the awakening it's a honor and blessing to know who I really am and also know that I am walking in the right direction led by the Holy Ruach.

Now you know I have to thank my beautiful wife of 24 years Shirley Diane Crutchfield for encouraging and her straight forward honesty about the poems I present to her. She's straight no chase about her criticism about my poems, I love her insight and criticism about the poems I present to her.

And to my two sons Brian and Dominique I love both of you two.

TABLE OF CONTENTS

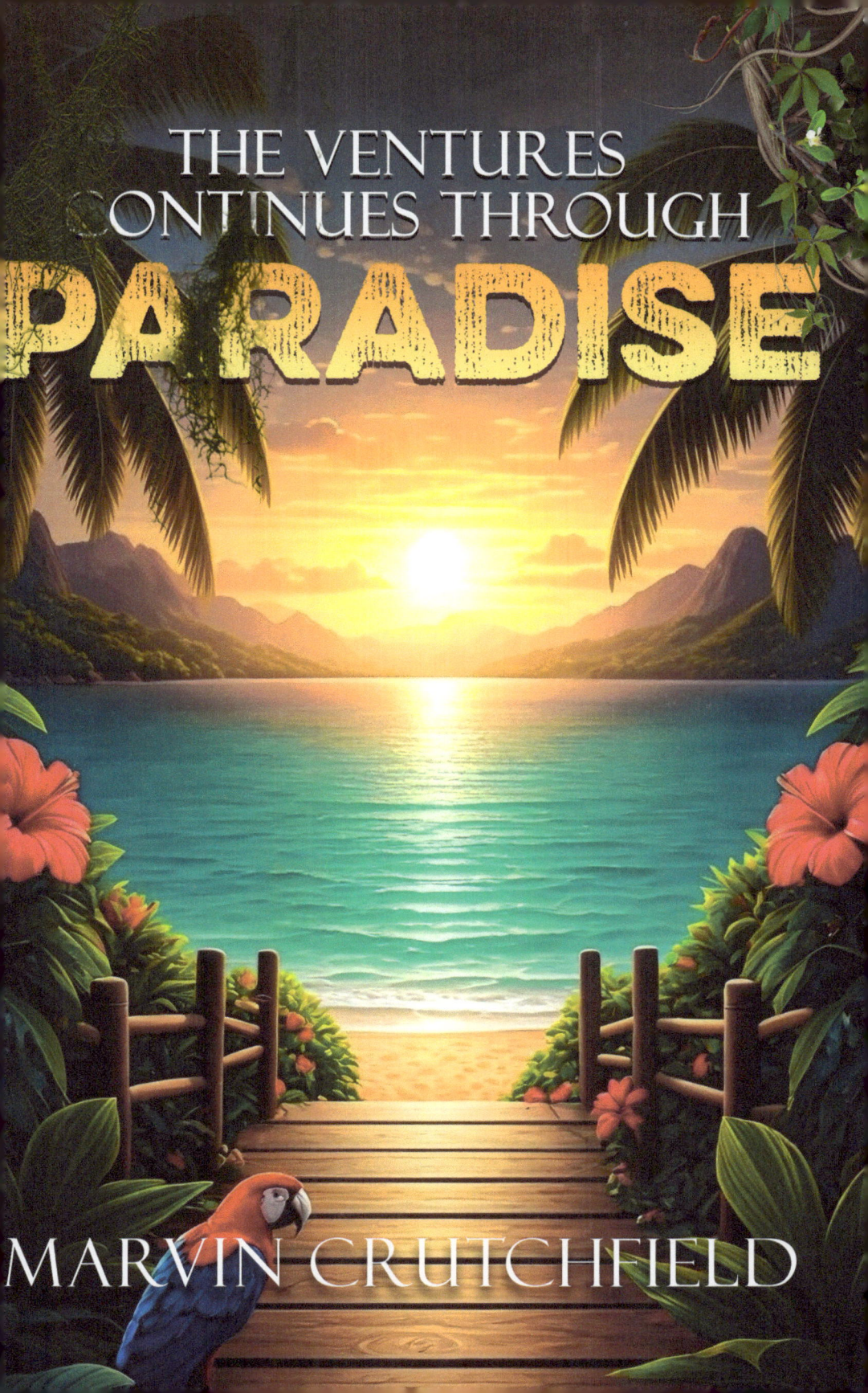

19

Caught on video in disguise
You were exposed for your hypocrisy and lies
Those that took the shot are now hooked to a machine
Injected with the number 19
19 represents the letter s
s stands for satan and stress
There is now nothing you can do
You volunteered yourself to be part of his crew
Because you listened to the media mass
And took the vaccine in a dash
Inspite of all the alarms
You fell victim to the government's charm
Or to their scare tactics
To make your life very drastic
Robin Williams once said nano nano
Well now that chip is in you

written by Marvin Crutchfield aka Mr Poetry

211

Let me tell you about the drink 211
It's part of the enemy's lethal weapon
Don't you know that's the penal code for robbery
Why is it targeted specifically for our community
Because where I live it is mostly blacks
I hope they know it's liquified crack
211 robs your brain cells
And in the morning have you feeling not so well
So that means it served it's purpose
To make you feel worthless
So remember if you keep drinking it with no hesitation
You're supporting the people who wants to destroy our black nation

written by Marvin Crutchfield aka Mr Poetry

A GHOST

You brag and boast
Now you're looking at a ghost
The murder you did is now a silhouette
What you see is what you get
You went off and flaunted
But now you are being haunted
Got you looking behind every door
Something you can't ignore
You can't even close your eyes
Because you can see that innocent man cries
Your spirit can't get any rest
Until you go and confess
But instead of turning yourself in
You go and commit a suicidal sin
You took a coward's way out
And chose hell no doubt

written by Marvin Crutchfield aka Mr Poetry

A HEART BEAT

I guess it's true what they say
Death is but a heart beat away
I was dead on arrival
With no chance of survival
So they covered me with the white sheet
But later on they heard a faint beep
While I was heavily sedated
I ascended to a heavenly ated
Yah says it's not your time
Trust me and everything will be fine
I said King can I stay here with You
And enjoy this eternal heavenly view
He says I need you to go back down there
And show the people that I really care
And with that I was back in the hospital bed
My King Yah had saved me from the dead

written by Marvin Crutchfield aka Mr Poetry

A PREACHER

Ask a preacher to do a sermon for free
Watch you get cussed out in the third degree
He will clear his throat and say
I need my cut for the day
I can't let that slide
I need my offerings and tithes
I got to keep my lavish lifestyle of living
So I'm gonna need all of y'all giving
Why you think I strut, hoop and holler
Cause I love that all American dollar
Even though the Word is free
I convinced the people to give to me
I know times are very hard
But sister so and so
Did you bring your ATM card
Just hurry up in a dash
And go to the machine in the lobby to get the cash
I'm worst than Creflo
Because no amount is too low

written by Marvin Crutchfield aka Mr Poetry

A RIOT

My mouth can start a riot
Because I will never be quiet
There's no way to shut me up
Because I don't give a fuck
Only way to bring me down
Is by a sharp metal round
Aka known as a bullet
But who got the guts to pull it
Because I fear no man
I will keep writing against their evil plan
With them I am heartless and bold
Because they are icy cold
I got to do whatever it takes
Keep writing until my pen breaks
Let this world know
This is not for the slow
It's moving at a fast pace
Because they are constantly lying to your face
I guess they forgot whose on the Throne
It's our King Yah who never left us alone
He's coming at a moment's notice
Because these distractions wants us to lose focus

written by Marvin Crutchfield aka Mr Poetry

A WOMAN'S PERSPECTIVE

The euphoric intensity
When you enter into me
It will be the ultimate climax
Like a train that stays on track
Headed straight for this love cave
Tuning me into your love slave
Yes baby I love your 10 inch pipe
It feels so good and it's so right
Yes I'm anticipating a liquid water fall
That will have me at your beck and call
So come over and lay in the bed
And let this wet mouth give you head
You satisfy my every need
So it will be a pleasure to have your seed
Because with you I can't get enough
Why you think you awoke in handcuffs

written by Marvin Crutchfield aka Mr. Poetry

ATONEMENT DAY

This day has arrived
Where our King Yah has exposed our enemy and his lies
It's atonement day
So now our enemy must pay
It's time for our King to avenge
Payback time called revenge
Revenge is definitely in His hands
Gonna strike terror and fear on this land
So be very afraid
Because our King Yah you can't evade
His mighty army his standing at attention
Waiting on His call to make earth's descending
Now the ultimate highlight
Is that He is with His people the Israelites
This is what we've been waiting for
Now our enemies are shaken to the core

Written by Marvin Crutchfeld aka Mr poetry

BANK RECEIPT

For those that took the vaccine
All that's left is for them is to turn on the machine
It's like a bank receipt
But your deposit was deceit
You no longer have control
You let your humanity be stole
Your injection was a nano chip
All it took was a snip
Now we will see in the long run
When life will no longer be fun
It looks good on the surface
But watch the metamorphosis
When you start to feel strange
Look in mirror and watch the change
You say I never felt better
But I didn't read my disclosure letter
When things start to fall apart
Damn I was deceived from the start

written by Marvin Crutchfield aka Mr Poetry

BLACK CARD

I forgot you're o massa's side
Your love for him you can't hide
Kanye turn in your black card
because you sound like a motherfucking retard
talking about slavery was a choice
when our people didn't have an opinion to voice
like bondage, torture and murder they would choose
not to mention the countless family members they would lose
so they chose to be slaves
and mistreated for 400 years and in the end put in a grave
never had a moment of peace
their only options were death and deceased
Kanye you say yes sir when whitey calls you nigger
so before you speak next time, get a gun
open your mouth and pull the trigger

written by Marvin Crutchfield aka Mr. Poetry

BLACK CARD 2

Kanye West always talking shit
Like our ancestors just ran and jumped on the slave ship
To be beaten down to the bone
And whipped so bad then left alone
Blood dripping down their skin
Just picturing this should make you cringe
Forced to eat on animal's slop
Lick it up like a mop
Chained and sold for the highest bid
And we suppose to forget this shit they did
According to Kanye this was our choice
Screamed as we were beaten as we lost our voice
We know you wanna be white
You hate yourself because your skin is not bright
Whitey laughs because you wanna be like him
Kanye start your procedure like lil Kim
Then you can really say massa we sick
His response is just keep sucking my dick

written by Marvin Crutchfield aka Mr. Poetry

B.L.A.C.K

Y'all know the deal
These crooked cops feel
They can kill us at will
And at this going rate
They will have caused our race to dissipate
By letting their drugs infiltrate
That means we approve of their hate
But we should put it down and take heed
Or we will affect Yah's seed with deformities
They have been plotting since our birth
How can we get rid of them from this earth
But it's not just them all the time
We've been made to turn against our own kind
But we should look back on where it all begin
And realize it came from the author of sin
So let's take a different route
Or we won't find what's heaven about

written by Marvin Crutchfield aka Mr Poetry

BLOODY TEARS

It's hard to maintain
These thoughts that are circling in my brain
It seems I can't get no rest
Got me thinking about this rotten mess
Face full of bloody tears
Because of the oncoming fears
Yes the fear of the unknown
Making himself very known
But we're living in revelation
The world is under a satanic sedation
The last days are right before our eyes
So these conspiracy theories are no surprise
Just like 911 when America threw the rock and hid their hands
This is some more sinister shit known to man
We better stop sleep walking
Because it's time for action and no more talking

written by Marvin Crutchfield aka Mr. Poetry

BOWEL'S WASTE

Since it was their plan to make us dissipate
Let's give them the same level of hate
How does those whips and chains feel
To be a moment away from murder, death, kill
Can't drink from that water fountain
Thinking about all that money I'm counting
You were the oppressor, now you're the oppressed
Your life is filled with grief and stress
Now we're the crooks on patrol
Shooting you up and have you dying in the cold
Your babies are tortured and maimed
Now their life will never be the same
How does it feel to watch your loved ones get sold
To a taskmaster who is heartless and cold
Now can you get a fucking clue
Of all the shit y'all put us through
How does that medicine taste
Because y'all worst than a pig's bowel waste

written by Marvin Crutchfield aka Mr Poetry

BRING IT ON

You better bring your whole team of SWAT
Because I'm gonna give you all that I've got
Yes this is reincarnated Turner Nat
I got AK's rocket launchers and Gats
What y'all thought I was dead
I'm back to put y'all crackers to bed
I'm America's worst nightmare
An educated black man who is strapped and doesn't care
My plan will be strategic
No more pledging to the motherfucking allegiance
Amerikka is full of shit
From day one
The black man always been hit
During my killing spree, I will not be calm
Because y'all are the one's who created this ticking time bomb
And to give y'all a taste of your own medicine
To be murdered by y'all own weapons

written by Marvin Crutchfield aka Mr Poetry

CLEAN SLATE

Why is the melinated man made to feel rejected
Then be thrown into the system
Where he will be misrepresentated
Then eventually he is incarcerated
I'm not making excuses because we're a minority
But why do we make up the majority in prison
Because some of us made the wrong decision
But when we're released and try to do what's right
Our past has become our plight
But we've got Yah now
And He has shown us the light
Although the world may still treat us mean
Our Yahuah has wiped our slate clean

written by Marvin Crutchfield aka Mr Poetry

COLOR FIRST

You can't tell me that these cops don't see color first
Because it's always a black man dying and put in a Hearst
Meanwhile a white boy can have a gun
The cops cause they think it's fun
He doesn't even get tazed
They justify it
by saying oh he's just going through a faze
It's called mental issues
They cry with him as they give him some tissue
I never heard of such a thing
Taking a killer to burger king
He used his privilege which was white
The cops assured him that everything will be alright
Yes they are to blame
It makes you wonder how are they trained
What's really on that course
Kill a nigga and show no remorse

written by Marvin Crutchfield aka Mr Poetry

DANDRUFF

In Yah we all can trust
Because He will shake the devil
Off you like a speck of dust
The enemy is like a patch of dandruff
By having you scratch your head
In a world of confusion
Because what he's offering you
Is nothing but an illusion
Be careful because he has all the tricks of the trade
To get you to be his eternal slave
So let Yah wash him away
like head and shoulders
Because in the end
Yah is going to crush him like boulders

written by Marvin Crutchfield aka Mr Poetry

DEFEATED

When the enemy sends his imps on assignment
Against Yah's immortal giants
But when they return
They will say mission was incomplete
Because we couldn't compete
We were overwhelmingly defeated by Yahuah our Lord
Because all of His people were of one accord
Since we couldn't infiltrate any traces of hate
We were sent back to our gate
A defeat we couldn't avoid
Because in the end
We knew that we were going to be destroyed

written by Marvin Crutchfield aka Mr. Poetry

DEMONIC DISGUISE

Now that we gave them a holiday
It's easier for us to make them sway
Every holiday what do niggas do
They say let's have a bbq
Spending their money with the enemy
Knowing that we are not friendly
We dress up in our demonic disguise
And keep serving them hate and lies
Look at them having fun with music and gigs
While eating a plate full of ribs
We got them thinking it's all well and fine
While eating an abomination called swine
Taking all of their wealth
While inflicting them with diseases and bad health
We got them to sin against Yah the Creator
While we remain the ultimate hater

written by Marvin Crutchfied aka Mr Poetry

EJACULATE

Some like to ejaculate
Others called it masturbate
Either way you're seeking a release
Not knowing you're sexing a beast
In your mind you're picturing an image
Letting yourself be diminished
Because you're doing self play
But you're actually doing self decay
It feels good for the moment
Only Yah can give you an atonement
Cause those demons love to play with your mind
Getting you to do acts that are unkind
Now after the wicked deed is done
They tricked you into thinking you had fun
But you just sexed up a demon
That was only after your semen

written by Marvin Crutchfield aka Mr Poetry

FALSE BELIEF

They call Yahuah Son of man
They call satan son of sam
Both have a voice
Both give you a choice
But who are you gonna listen to
One loves you unconditionally
The other gives you false love with conditions
Yahuah really cares
While satan is the prince of the air
satan causes confusion
While everything he gives you is an illusion
Christianity was the best drug on the market
That's why the melinated people were the targets
Just like crack cocaine
It was hard for the people to restrain
One hit got the people hooked
So the people believed everything coming from the book
Even though the preacher was lying through his teeth
He was still able to cast the people into a false belief

written by Marvin Crutchfield aka Mr Poetry

FATAL THOUGHTS

These thoughts of mine be scattered
It's like fragments of brain splatter
They be all over the place
Like a junkie mixing heroin and cocaine base
Now I have no control
Sexual demons trying to snatch my soul
Like the frequencies of brain waves
Fantasies of other women I wanna crave
But it's like crashing into a wall
Setting me up for a fatal fall
It's like I jumped out of a plane without a parachute
Landing on wires and got electrocuted
Now I'm laying in a hospital bed
Spiritually frightened and almost dead
Looked up and saw my beautiful wife
Whose staying by my side through death and life

written by Marvin Crutchfield aka Mr Poetry

FRIEND OF MINE

At first I let the enemy lead me astray
Until Yah showed me a better way
He said you should make a choice
And then listen to your inner voice
He said I will never lead you into temptation
But you'll face trial and tribulation
He said with Him I can't lose
Just stay with Him and don't refuse
That's why I thank Him for keeping me
And saving me from that fiery sea
That's why I know in the end
He will always be my eternal friend
He said if I keep playing this game of sin
That's a game I will never win
Because everyone who tried lost
And eventually had to pay the cost
Because it's your life I wanna save
And keep from being the enemy's slave

written by Marvin Crutchfield aka Mr Poetry

FROM DREAM TO REALITY

I got to make my dream a reality
So it won't be a regret causality
In my dream I can see the vision
So I have to be on a mission
To keep my desire and passion
To make it everlasting
It's in my right hand
So I won't tell my left
Because if I do it will lead to dream death
Since Yah knows my heart
He says keep it from the agents of the dark
He says give it to Him to hide in the secret place
And it will come to fruition at the appropriate date

GIFT

From Yahuah I received this gift
That's keeping me well equipped
With the weapons I need to fight
Things that are out of my sight
He's keeping me from falling apart
And from eternal dark
He sealed this poem on my heart
He saved me from dark forces
Kept me on the right courses
Because He has remorse
You know the enemy pretends to be
Just as twice as nice
But take Yah's advice
That's a trick for you to drop your jab
So he can inflict that fatal stab
So I'm staying with Yah the Lord
Because I can't afford
To clown around
And lose my soul underground

written by Marvin Crutchfield aka Mr Poetry

Go

It will be time for the big show
Once our King and Creator Yah says go
Yes it will on and popping
And there will be no stopping
Chaos and mass destruction
Angels will be revenging all of earth's corruption
Michael and Gabriel taking the lead
In protecting Yah's peculiar seeds
And for those that took the mark
Their mind and body can't prepare for this eternal dark
It will be all out revenge
Because Yah always keeps His word to avenge
Got the people shaking like a leaf
Because they are still in shock and disbelief
They can't believe what's happening right before their eyes
Because they were not prepared for their own demise

written by Marvin Crutchfield aka Mr Poetry

GUILTY

During your trial you presented evidence
To try and get yourself heaven sent
But I know the real deal
That's why I have your life on a movie reel
From that surprised look on your face
You didn't have a word to say
As you were watching the movie screen
You thought the things you did were unseen
You forgot that I have eyes everywhere
As you can see, you never had a care
From all the hurt that you caused
You never took a moment to pause
And think about the repercussions
That you left a lot of people suffering
But now that you are standing in front of Me (YAH)
I find you guilty in the first degree

written by Marvin Crutchfield aka Mr Poetry

HEY COP

Hey cop how does it feel
to be on the other side of murder, death, kill
You had all the evidence
Video footage of everything was present
But a jury of his peers says he was justified
Even though we all know it was homicide
He was able to walk away scott free
On a minor technicality
Now as a cop you get full honors
But your family mourns you as a goner
Your family says how can this be
The court found him innocent
but in his he knew he was guilty
The death was very horrific
Cold blooded, calculated and specific
The gun never made a sound
Shot by a silencer
His body was dead before he even hit the ground

written by Marvin Crutchfield aka Mr Poetry

HOODIES

Hey klan I wear hoodies too
But I don't hide my face like you do
My hoodies have all kinds of designs
Yours is a warning sign
Mines says I'm not afraid
You only wear yours in a group to go on a raid
Underneath you're a scared lil bitch
Yeah you Peter, Bobby and Mitch
But remember we all bleed the same
Oh and last time I checked bullets have no name
I know most of y'all are in high places
That's why y'all can't show your faces
But y'all already have been exposed
Because on judgement day
Y'all will be naked without any clothes

written by Marvin Crutchfield aka Mr poetry

HOW COME

Like a cow that loves to graze
How these evil people never paid for their evil ways
Like a dog that loves to bark
How com these evil people love to lurk in the dark
Like a snake that loves to hiss
How come we got people that puts up with this
Like a shark that senses blood
How come we got to drown because of sin's flood
Like a bird that flies in the air
How come the people of this world don't care
Like a bear that eats all the honey
How come they think people's misfortunes are funny
Like a ant that loves to build
How come all these people think about is murder, death and kill
Like a horse that eats hay
These people will never escape judgement day

writtten by Marvin Crutchfield aka Mr. Poetry

I STILL TRUST YOU

I feel the pain from my ancestors soul
When from their land they were stole
All I can do is cry
Some were captured and some had to die
Ok whitey I trust you after you guinea pig me at Tuskegee
Ok whitey I still trust you after slavery
Ok whitey I still you after black wall st.
Ok whitey I still trust you after you raped our men and women
Ok whitey I still trust you after you used our babies as alligator bait
Ok whitey I still trust you after you murdered me and my loved ones
Ok whitey I still trust you after you beat me
Ok whitey I still trust you after you constantly rob me
Ok whitey I still trust you after you put drugs in our communities
Ok whitey I still trust you after you false imprison me
Ok whitey I still trust you after you lie after lie after lie
Ok whitey I still trust you after you said Jesus was white
but whitey I'm tired of your lies this vaccine is the last straw
I can't trust you anymore unless I'm just plain stupid and dumb to keep
trusting you

written by Marvin Cruthfield aka Mr Poetry

IF

If that was my daughter
They would've prepared for a slaughter
Shots rang out boom boom
His body would be dead in the court room
Brains would have been splattered everywhere
Because at that point and time
I don't care
Klan member made it that much sweeter
Now he's in his own blood sinking deeper
Yes he played a crazy role
Now he can be with his father satan
To whom he sold his soul

written by Marvin Crutchfield aka Mr Poetry

INSANE

So you wanna call me insane
But you're the one who let them wash your brain
It's on every screen
Come and get your vaccine
It's on every dash
Now your brain reacts to every flash
Now you're hypnotized
Cause you fell for their lies
They said it will cause no harm
You took the bait like a junkie with a needle in his arm
You took that lethal dose
Because you thought death was coming close
But that was just a smoke screen
To see if you are really keen
But I'm supposed to be the crazy one
For realizing what they have done

written by Marvin Crutchfield aka Mr poetry

JEOPARDY

I apologize for causing your family cries
I apologize cause I know it's me you despise
I apologize for doing dirt
I apologize for all the hurt
I apologize for the rapes
I apologize for the hate
I apologize for the kills
I apologize because it's happening still
I apologize for tearing your families apart
I apologize for my cold black heart
I apologize for making you a slave
I apologize because I'm still a coward and never brave
I apologize for my generation
I apologize for your frustrations
I apologize for all the pain
I apologize even though it's all in vain

written by Marvin Crutchfield aka Mr. Poetry

JUNE 18TH

This system is an epic fail
That got people of color wagging their tails
They threw us a bone
So we can leave them alone
Let's make it a federal holiday
That way they will have nothing to say
The 18th of June
While we plot their oncoming destruction soon
What about reparations
Yeah right!
We still causing their own separation
We will never give them a crime bill
We are making too much off them with murder, death and kill
If not we got their own kind
Pushing our agenda to control their minds
Yes they see them as leaders
When actually they are our bottom feeders

written by Marvin Crutchfield aka Mr Poetry

KICKING IT

While you were out there kicking it in the clubs
Your time was running without any subs
Out on the streets shooting dice
All the time you put Yah on ice
Shots rang out very loud
Next you know you're in the clouds
Talking to Yah One on one
He said I wanted to save you
But you were too busy rejecting My Son (Yahuah)
Before those bullets pierced your chest
I wanted you to be different an the rest
But since you did no repentance
Read the sign: It says no admittance

written by Marvin Crutchfield aka Mr Poetry

LAND OF LUNATICS

Welcome to the land of lunatics
They wanna put us all in the matrix
Offering us a red or blue pill
To keep us on a hallucinated thrill
Believing in stuff that's not there
While they continuing to work for the prince o the air
Like a junkie on a binge
Up next is this poisonous vaccinated syringe
I mean what is your level of comprehension
Crooked cops get to murder and get a paid suspension
We will never get any satisfaction
But we can anticipate the next distraction
Rest assured the next one will be dramatic
Like a volcano that is climatic
Ready to explode
To watch them continually treating us
heartless and cold

written by Marvin Crutchfield aka Mr Poetry

LICKING HIS CHOPS

satan probably licking his chops
because his evil entity of people never stops
You got molesters, murderers and thieves
loving seeing the people grieve
Look at him as he salivates
Because all around the world is his message of hate
But he knows his time is ticking
he's preparing for his eternal ass kicking
So he's doing all that he can
To destroy every woman, child and man
Get them confused of their gender
Saying it's ok to be a transgender
So he designed a whole community of lesbians and gays
So he can lead them astray
They have totally disobeyed Yah our King
But are they ready for a sad ending

written by Marvin Crutchfield aka Mr Poetry

LOOK

Look what this world has become
People are heartless and numb
Their hearts are gross waxed cold
Everyone including the young and old
It feels like wasted years
Makes me wanna cry a bucket of tears
All this is happening for a reason
It's just that time of season
Yah all we can do
Is put our hope and trust in You
You already told us about the warning signs
The fall and destruction of mankind
man has become full of pride
Allowed evil entities to creep inside
They have become their own obsession
And let themselves be a demonic possession
But my King Yah will restore
And this will not be ignored
Yah's people will inherit this earth
The way Yah intended from our birth

written by Marvin Crutchfield aka Mr Poetry

LOVE SCENE

If my thoughts were a crime
I would be locked up doing major time
These thoughts are very deceiving
Especially if I'm entertaining them and receiving
Because that's a spirit and it's demonic
Thoughts are coming faster than the game called sonic
Take me for prime example
The enemy is trying to use me as a sample
Got me thinking thoughts of lust
About another woman's vagina to bust
Like an volcanic eruption
These thoughts are seducing and seduction
Just like the song called love scene
These thoughts are too explicit for the tv screen
Like a dope fiend that needs his narcotic
These thoughts are just too erotic
My thoughts are a drama filled reality show
But I must shut them down and tell them no
At all cost I must lose it's grip
Or I will definitely be falling in that pit

written by Marvin Crutchfield aka Mr Poetry

MADNESS AND INSANITY

With all this madness and insanity
Biden and his crew
should be charged with crimes against humanity
All of his old ass cronies
Are nothing but fake ass phonies
Now he wanna issue a mandate
He wants you to comply and vaccinate
Take away their way to live
And depend on us to give
No job or wages
So if they steal we can lock them up in our cages
Keep them under a mental slave ship
To be controlled by dictatorship
All orchestrated by the prince of the air
And we know that satan never will care
Because we lied to them about health
When the bottom line it was all our wealth

written by Marvin Crutchfield aka Mr Poetry

MY ANCESTORS

I can hear my ancestors marching
Along with their dogs barking
Yes we love the chase
Putting fear on y'all pale white faces
Chase y'all into the woods
Cause y'all were up to no good
Tie y'all up on a tree
Damn it feels so good to me
Now y'all are really stuck
And we really don't give two fucks
Beat y'all to a bloody pulp
But the pain you can't really cope
Force y'all to change your name
Bringing your whole race to shame
See that blood that's dripping from your back
This is just a preview of the big payback
That's something y'all can't picture
But y'all can't run from the scriptures

written by Marvin Crutchfield aka Mr Poetry

MY THOUGHTS

Because of Yah I maintain
If not for Him,
I would be locked up with the criminally insane
Yah is the One who gives me rest
While I'm here on earth taking this test
Sometimes my thoughts shift to the left
Thinking about nothing but hate and death
Yes I let them roam
But Yah always brings me back home
They seem so captivating
and so fascinating
If my thinking was a crime
I'd be locked up until the end of time
Or strapped to a chair
Because at times I simply don't care
Rather thinking evil or good
I try to be as neutral the best way I could
My thoughts need a straight jacket
Or a suit case so I can pack it

written by Marvin Crutchfield aka Mr. Poetry

MY(STRESS)

Don't you know it's a risky business
Being someone's mistress
Be careful because what he's offering you
Are a lot of shattered dreams and broken promises
By messing with him what have you accomplished
All you did was destroy a once solid relationship
How would you feel if you were on the other side of it
All this time he had a loving, caring and faithful wife
But you two are bringing her misery and strife
Next thing you know she's having a nervous breakdown
Because her husband is sleeping around town
She forgave both of you before her demise
Now she's with Yah and watching the sunrise

written by Marvin Crutchfield aka Mr Poetry

NO BARS

You duped the world into a false belief
So you were able to become a master thief
The world never heard of ya
So it was easy for you to become a mass murderer
Like a cat burglar that likes to creep
Evil and crime are what you seek
You have never cared
That's why you like your meat medium rare
A blood taste has always been your desire
So you'll do anything that's required
Human or animal parts
It makes no difference because you have no heart
You always cast chaos and confusion
The false love you gave was an illusion
Let's rewind the time
And show y'all life of crime
Cause it seems like y'all just don't get it
But you want us to forget it
We have been permanently scarred
We're walking prisoners with no bars
We will never be free
As long as we are enslaved mentally

written by Marvin Crutchfield aka Mr Poetry

NO ESCAPE

Rather you agree or disagree
You will stand before Almighty Me (Yah)
Yah stands for Yah always here
I'm The One whom y'all should fear
There will be no escape
Because I am Yah the great
You can go to the deepest end of the earth
You can't hide because I've known you before your birth
satan is the prince of the air
As you can see he will never care
And yet people still do his bidding
And go against Me on what I say is forbidden
They bow down to his will
To plot, scheme, murder and kill
But everyone will answer My call
When they face their final fall (die)

written by Marvin Crutchfield aka Mr Poetry

NO MYSTERY

I guess we won't get any reparations
Cause they have been robbing us for centuries and generations
Y'all hire crooks to patrol the land
To continue to leave carnage of the black man
Crooked cops see us and don't hide
They laugh as they murder black males for genocide
Something about that uniform it brings out the worst
Because we're like targets that they shoot first
Back in the day we got hung and made a public spectacle
Dicks cut off and a pole stuck in our rectal
Betrayal is their game
They do this shit everyday without shame
Evil and treachery is their history
It's who they are so it's no mystery

written by Marvin Crutchfield aka Mr Poetry

NOT EVEN HUMAN

Y'all not even human
Y'all just a beast from the cave
The sun is your enemy
that's why you captured us as slaves
Your skin can't take the heat
That's why every chance you get
my people you would beat
Damn this jealousy is way past skin deep
It's amazing y'all motherfuckers can even sleep
Y'all came with evil intent
And everyday y'all are hell bent
But y'all need us to survive
Because without us y'all would surely die
That's why y'all love to mix breed
So your babies can be a melanated seed
Because your body needs this precious melanin
That was only made for us and our skin

written by Marvin Crutchfield aka Mr. Poetry

NOT YOUR AVERAGE

I'm not your average
Keep fucking with me
I will turn into a mode of savage
And tear you apart
Rip out your feeble heart
It depends on the time of day
Yes I can get CRA CRA
They say music calms the savage beast
But it's too late my fury has been released
Now you wanna change your tune
Because you saw changing at the full moon
Now I got you shook
Because I am the Werewolf
Coming at you full throttle
To tuck you in
And give you a baby's bottle
Put your punk ass to sleep
From all those tears that you weeped

written by Marvin Crutchfield aka Mr Poetry

OBITUARY POST

Black face turned into a ghost
Last seen on a obituary post
Put there by a crooked cop
His crimes will never stop
The loved one's get to read
Expressions from their dying seed
The words are in black ink
Reading them made their hearts sink
Because this is all that's left
Never to be seen again, because of life theft
I guess it was his fate
But I never thought that I would lose him
because of hate.

Written by Marvin Crutchfield aka Mr Poetry

OUR PLAN

Through addiction or extermination
Our plan is working to rid blacks from this nation
From our cotton fields and slave ships
To poisoning of their water
or the music that's called hip
To locking them up in the pen
Or let them kill each other like a savage beast
in the lion's den
The females have no education, so they aren't working
but somehow they have a master's degree in smoking weed and twerking
Oh yes we love to corrupt their seed
by raping them to have a mixed breed
We're the masters of manipulation
every since we stepped foot on USA's foundation.

Written by Marvin Crutchfield aka Mr Poetry

OUT OF TIME

Life is like looking at the sand in the hourglass
Wondering how long will it last
It starts out going slow
And have you thinking I've ot a long way to go
So you say I'm going to just take time
In deciding what to do with this life of mine's
So you finally come to an conclusion
But it's too late
Because now your life is nothing but an illusion
so you say what are you talking about
Yah showed you the hourglass
and said your time is out

written by Marvin Crutchfield aka Mr Poetry

OWN BACKYARD

I guess he had a bad day as well
And decided to make ten families suffer to a living hell
Was it too much stress
He murdered a cop in the process
But he was able to survive
Walked out peacefully alive
America raises terrorists for fun
But a black would have had a different outcome
Body shot full of holes
Blood would have been leaking out of control
America is too busy searching for terrorists afar
But they ignore the fact
that they are right here in their own backyard
Case in point the klan and crooked cops
Their terrorists ways will never stop

written by Marvin Crutchfield aka Mr. Poetry

PAIN

As the years passed, the pain has subsided
With the vivid memories
Of you running to the screen door
With tears in your eyes
Wondering why were we leaving
Maybe it was way of mom how you treated
So after we piled up in the car
And drove away very far
After we settled here out west
I was hoping you would come to your senses and do what's best
Come and raise your boys to be a man
But I see you had different plans
You were trapped in a disease called women and alcohol
That was the cause of your fall
You know what really hurts
Is that you passed down a generational curse
But Yah knew that type of lifestyle I wouldn't fit
He said call on Him if I wanna break it
As a man I will never run
Because Yah is helping me raise my sons

written by Marvin Crutchfield aka Mr Poetry

PLAN B

Adam you did what you did
Then try to cover it up and hid
Oh you blamed your mate sister Eve
Now you cursed the generations with grieve
Remember Yah gave you specific instructions
Now it was you who caused earth's destruction
You have released this insidious sin
That we currently live and dwell in
Every day we face temptation
Evil looks good with it's persuasions
Because evil was just too much
That's why Yah said don't even touch
Because evil can overtake you
Use you up and then you are through
But Yah already had a Plan B
To save us all for eternity

written by Marvin Crutchfield aka Mr Poetry

PLANET VENUS

I'm in this grand arena
Sitting next to Venus and Serena
I looked around and saw all these stars
Then I realized it was planet Hollywood at the bar
But Venus is a planet like no other
She's a bona-fide freak under cover
Her pussy was a hot flame
Begging to be tamed
We went about three or four sets
She took all what she can get
She said oh let me polish that knob
Because I love to slob
She said I love all this cum
Too bad my sister can't have none
Then she hollered game, set, match
I got a plane to catch

written by Marvin Crutchfield aka Mr Poetry

POSTER BOY

So how is it being satan's poster boy
Yeah he gave you a few toys
Yes these are your worldly possessions
Now they will be your obsession
Every day you will crave more
That's what I chose you for
Because I know you salivate for money and greed
So I just planted that seed
You may think you have heart
But in reality you're surrounded by agents of the dark
You love to boast and brag
But if you don't come back to Yahuah
The ending for you will be very sad

written by Marvin Crutchfield aka Mr Poetry

PUSHING UP DAISIES

You just had to fuel my anger
That's why you caught those bullets from the chamber
Put your ass six feet deep
Now all of hell is yours to keep
Cause you came in the wrong house
And tried to creep around like a mouse
But in store for you was a nice surprise
When that boom boom caused your untimely demise
Now you're dearly departed
From the evil that you started
When you did a unlawful break-in and entry
But your ending wasn't so friendly
Now you're pushing up daisies
Because you wanted to be crazy
But it just cost you your life
Now you're in eternal darkness and no light

written by Marvin Crutchfield aka Mr Poetry

THE RED CARPET

That red carpet is a sea of blood
It swallows lives up without any love
Look at them striking a pose
Walking like puppets without control
There are no strings attached
Only demons there to attack
They hear their shoes going squish squish
Now they bow down to the baphomet for their wish wish
he says look up you are now a star
Stick with me and you will get far
Look at that walk of fame
Can't you just envision your name
All the power and prestige
For a small favor and a fee
Look at this card deck
Make sure you do a thorough check
Now sit back and watch me deal
Remember I play to have fun and thrills
So sign write here
Don't worry you have nothing to fear
Oh my ace in the hole
You just sold me your soul
(satan cackles)

written by Marvin Crutchfield aka Mr Poetry

FINE PRINT (PART 2 OF RED CARPET)

I see you didn't read that fine print
Let me show you what I really meant
Yes that's your John Hancock
My deception never stops
Pull back the curtain
Now one thing is for certain
Look at that wall of fame
I mean the wall of shame
Those are the people that I despised
I double crossed them when they looked into my eyes
They are now my fallen stars
They thought it was the limelight, but it was really dark
They did whatever it takes
Even bowed down to me the snake
My deception was very discreet
They thought that they were exempt
Because they were part of the elite
Y'all are my biggest clientele
Because y'all never think about afterlife in HELL

written by Marvin Crutchfield aka Mr Poetry

PART 3 RED CARPET

Now look at these souls that I collected
Yeah the elite and selected
Too late to rewrite the script
They are forever taking a fiery dip
Lights camera action
All done for my satisfaction
They all smiled when those cameras flashed
But their life was over in a dash

written by Marvin Crutchfield aka Mr Poetry

REJECTION

If you could see what's going on inside
Mama I'm trying to find a place to hide
From all the smoke that I'm receiving
How could a mom be so deceiving
Mom what if I come out deformed
Then you'll wish I never was born
I thought a mom's job was for protection
And not for rejection
Mom it's your love that I need
And I won't get it from no weed
So please do yourself a good deed
And let Yah be your lead

written by Marvin Crutchfield aka Mr Poetry

RESULTS

Mama what are you going to do when I start teething
Or when I have problems with my breathing
You can't blame no one but yourself
Because I'm having problems with my health
Mom I wanna avoid this lifetime of misery
That you know you're causing me
Mom I'm want you to hear this
Because I'm talking from my spirit
Mom I love you dearly
I just want you to see the picture more clearly

written by Marvin Crutchfield aka Mr Poetry

RIOT

These crazy folks like to riot
Because they hate peace and quiet
But this shouldn't be a surprise
When the people that helped them has the same color blue eyes
This is how they demonstrate
Act ignorant and show hate
Terrorism is in their DNA
That's why to them it was just another day
Walking around with their chest out and acting bold
Summoning the spirits of their ancestors
who were also heartless and cold
That made them smile from the grave
Because that's how they acted untamed and wouldn't behave
Since they wrote the law
They can say Fuck the law
What a joke of the constitution
Knowing if the melinated people had done the same
They would've been locked up in their prison of institutions

written by Marvin Crutchfield aka Mr. Poetry

SEX

Like a pill in water that dissolves
I got Yahuah now, so my problem is solved
I got a demon on my brain
and her name is sex
Treating me like a prostitute and be like next
She's constantly on my mind
Showing me all these women of different kind
Like a smorgasbord or a buffet
Saying choose which one you wanna lay
I can see the vivid picture and it's clear
It's like I can touch it because it's near
Sex is saying make your choice
But now I hear this deeper voice
Saying you are all mine's
Has been since the beginning of time
Don't fall for satan's evil tactics
Because the end will be very drastic
Follow Me and make her your ex
And I will rid yo of that demon named sex

written by Marvin Crutchfield aka Mr Poetry

SHELL GAME

Their playing this game called shell
Trying to give you a one way ticket to hell
In a slick and sinister way
Got people in line everyday
They wanna make you a statistic
Because they are vile and sadistic
The truth is hidden in plain sight
People are dying without putting up a fight
This is no joke
Take that vaccine and you have no hope
People just do your research
Because they will lie and say it doesn't hurt
Don't be so naive
And just sit there and roll up your sleeve
And let them inject
The poison that will have an adverse effect

written by Marvin Crutchfield aka Mr Poetry

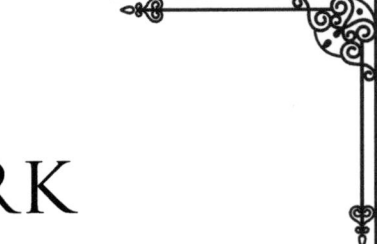

SMIRK

It usually comes with a smile or a smirk
But definitely some one will be murked
Because you went against the grain
Now they wanna inflict pain
Yes it's the illuminati
Plotting sinister shit that's naughty
They're like ravenous wolves eating on sheep
Because of the promises you didn't keep
Now everything you did with them will be exposed
Like you running around naked with no clothes
You didn't follow their game plan
Now it's time for them to assassinate your character as a man
The situation is a catch 22
Because there is nothing you can do
It's all on film
Chances of denying it are slim
It's an evil entity
There are a lot of ruined lives aplenty
So stay off their team
Because you will be left with heart in hand and a trail of blood stream

written by Marvin Crutchfield aka Mr. Poetry

SNAKE KING

I see this lustful demon
Trying to steal my semen
But because of King Yah I'm able to recognize
This snake aka king of lies
Giving me these illicit thoughts
Trying to stop me from thinking about the eternal cost
It was a smoked filled illusion
Blinding me from seeing the final conclusion
Yes my desired flesh
Would have been a scattered mess
It's like this demon is on my shoulder
Making my thoughts colder and colder
These thoughts are not from Yah my King
But from satan the snake king

written by Marvin Crutchfield aka Mr Poetry

S.O.S

It may be an awful situation
But I want a place of dedication
Somewhere out of the cold
But mostly a place to save my soul
Because this world surely acts funny
When you lose your job and run out of money
They will throw you out on the streets
Without shoes to put on your feet
You see I was once making major cash
But now I'm here sifting through the trash
But that's how fast the tables can turn
When you think that you have money to burn
In heaven I don't have to worry about none of this
Because I'll be with Yah and pure bliss

written by Marvin Crutchfield aka Mr Poetry

SPILLED TEA

When is our government ever to be trusted
Because of the evil stuff they do
One day they will be busted
There's a lot of tea to be spilled
That's why a lot of innocent people get killed
So my mouth I can't keep closed
Because their dark secrets have to be exposed
What really happens behind those closed doors
They plot evil all the more
All these demons sitting at the round table
Gathering their constituents like a prostitute's stable
What more sinister stuff can we plan
Cause all day we throw rocks and hide our hand
It's a table of the triple six
Looking for more pain to inflict
Let them take our vaccine
Because the effects will be be unseen
It all starts from the inside
That will cause a catastrophic genocide
But our King Yah has the final say
And they will not get away

written by Marvin Crutchfield aka Mr Poetry

TERRORISTS

We raise our fist in peace
But get shot up by terrorists (crooked cops)
Now we're deceased
What is it about our skin
That have y'all committing these atrocities of sin
It seems like it's embedded in y'all gene pool
To keep hating and acting a fool
What's on y'all crime bill
Put on a uniform to go nigga kill
Yes we are in a new era
Crooked cops are allowed to enforce their reign of terror
It's like a two-faced man
part crooked cop and part klan
This is someone we're supposed to trust
When they see black skin they love to cap bust
And these murdering acts will continue
Because black men will always be on their kill menu

written by Marvin Crutchfield aka Mr Poetry

THE BLACK MARKET

We're a walking commodity
That's why they want every part of our body
To them we're a cash cow
Why you think they killing us now
To our hair and skin and nails
They doing it without fail
And that is just the outside
Let's talk about the inside
They are taking every organ
The plan is going according
We getting set up like a butcher shop
They salivating on a black body they can chop
We will always be a target
While they sell our body parts on the black market
Oh by the way Melanin is on the stock exchange
So tell me, doesn't that feel strange

written by Marvin Crutchfield Aka Mr Poetry

THE DAMAGE

Y'all are so afraid of this awakening
So y'all can't no longer do any taking
Y'all done took everything we owned
Started when y'all kidnapped us from our home
Since day one y'all been poisoning the food we eat
Giving us old and rotted meat
Oh what about the water we drink
Making us sterile and losing our ability to think
Betraying my own race
But I got to love my enemy
and hate the one with my same colored face
Systematically we've been destroyed
Because we're treated like chess pieces moved around and used like toys
Congratulations our pyschy is through
For meeting a race (white) of people like you
It's a wonder that we still have our sanity
After the damage you've done to my people
who have the same skin color as me

written by Marvin Crutchfield aka Mr. Poetry

THE FIGHT OF THE CENTURY

Come one come all
Come watch the enemy fall
When he steps into the ring
With Our Heavenly King
He will shiver with fear
Because he knows the end is near
Yahuah will destroy him with one blow
In case you didn't know
This fight will be broadcasted all over the evening news
Because after satan watches the replay
he will say I always lose
The punch happened so fast
I didn't see it coming
I might as well kept on running
After I awoke from my comatose mind state
The fight was over
Now my eternal home is the burning lake
This is for the followers of satan
The news they are hearing is devastating
Because they looked up to their hero
But Yahuah has reduced him to an absolute zero

written by Marvin Crutchfield aka Mr Poetry

THE GOODNESS

I know she's all for it
Because the taste of her pussy will be euphoric
I want it dripping all down my chin
Some call eating out
But I prefer to dine in
Not a drop will go to waste
Because she's grinding it all on my face
She says gimme all that tongue
Because I am definitely getting sprung
Somebody definitely told a big fat lie
I guess they never gave pussy a try
Saying a dog is man's best friend
Cause I can eat pussy to no end
Especially when it's hot and wet
All that goodness I will get
Now watching those legs shake
Like a 7.0 earthquake

written by Marvin Crutchfield aka Mr Poetry

THE POETRY CUP

I feel like Yah is holding a cup in His hand
And pouring His poetry in this man (me)
Writing His poetry relieves my stress
And causes me to be very blessed
That's why I thank Him every day
For giving me the words to write and say
Because it's all true
And He will never lie to me or you
His poetry cup is filled to the rim
That's why I'm writing it
Because it's all from Him

written by Marvin Crutchfield aka Mr Poetry

THE STREAM

Can you picture Yahuah's blood trickling down a stream
Gathering up souls for eternal team
As the stream goes by
You see all those smiling faces
Because they know they're going to heavenly places
You're standing there contemplating should I jump in
Not realizing it will wash away your sins
You see your reflection in this stream
It's smiling back at you as it gleams
The inner part of you knows it's safe no doubt
Because it will be with the One with all clout
So you jump in and go for a swim
That was the best decision you ever made
Because you're eternally with HIM

written by Marvin Crutchfield aka Mr Poetry

THE UNSPOKEN

I speak for the unspoken
And I refuse to be a negro that's a token
Venom and vengeance runs through my veins
The madness I can't contain
Yes I thank my Creator Yah that I am alive
But back then with my mouth and attitude
I would not have survived
Best believe I would have put up a fight
Or if they caught
The ropes would have been extra tight
But since today I have a voice
I will use because it's my choice
I will never sell out, so you can't buy it
Death would be the only way to keep me quiet

written by Marvin Crutchfield aka Mr Poetry

THESE HOES

These hoes out here selling sex
You're so contaminated I don't even wanna text
Saying your pussy is tha bomb
But what it really needs is a douche and napalm
Even the crabs you have are under attack
Because all you do is scratch
You can't even hold your breath
Because your pussy smells like death
So do yourself a favor and wash it with comet
So the next man that you encounter don't hit the sink and vomit

written by Marvin Crutchfield aka Mr Poetry

TIME OUT

Time truly can be your friend
If you cherish it to the end
Time is like the precious air
Yah gives us because He cares
So treasure every breath
Because we all have a time of death
Eternity has no clock on the wall
The question is did you accept
Or hang up on Yah's call
Time is like a beautiful pearl
Value it before you leave this world
Stop treating it like garbage's waste
Because in the end you will see Yah's face
Now eternity's time has no numbers
Because Yah sees all
And He never sleeps nor slumber
Time doesn't care if you're poor or rich
Because all of us will get the same size ditch

written by Marvin Crutchfield aka Mr Poetry

TREASON

Blacks kills blacks for no reason
It's like committing ancestry treason
Young black males are dying to an early grave
It's a slap in the face
To the ones who were slaves
They already look at us as refuse
Why you think they smile every time a gun is used
One less of us is on the street
Just another piece of dead meat
Black man with his pants saggin
Thrown into the coroner's meat wagon
Hanging us with their ropes
Having us thinking we have no hope
That's why we have to kill them with our mind
Instead walking around deaf, dumb and blind
Beat them at their own game
And put their asses to shame
Reach for our highest goal
Stay with Yah and let Him take control
So our ancestors trial and tribulations won't be in vain
Now we can have joy instead of pain

written by Marvin Crutchfield aka Mr Poetry

TWO SHOTS

Just imagine all those people going through a struggle
Feels like they're stuck in a bubble
With no oxygen or any air
Cause the powers that be don't even care
Got these celebrities pushing this poisonous vaccine
Being insidious, heartless and mean
To them it's all about numbering
They could care less whose succumbing
Because death is the closest
If it doesn't happen then
They will increase the dosage
That's why they give you two shots
To make sure your insides rot
To them you're just a dollar sign
While leaving your loved ones crying
This is definitely not the norm
That's why they have you sign a disclosure form
The poison is not even properly tested
But best believe they have a lot of money invested

written by Marvin Crutchfield aka Mr Poetry

UNAPOLOGETIC

It's a shame that two of sisters stop speaking to me
All because of what I said about whitey aka the enemy
What I speak about them are true facts
Their past history confirms that
It seems like we will never reconcile
Because we haven't spoken in a while
Imagine if I had talked about them
Then my chances would be none or slim
They read what I say as hate
But these edomites have been evil from the gate
So what I speak is the truth
So why is there conflict between us too
But I still love them and I hope they get it
But my poetry will remain unapologetic
I hope one day that they will open their eyes
and really just recognize

written by Marvin Crutchfield aka Mr Poetry

WAKE UP

We better wake up and stop being black hearted
Before we be reading a obituary saying dearly departed
By then it will be too late
Because all that time we were being fake
The love that was given was false
Now we wanna regret our loss
Body in a casket or ashes in a urn
Now we wanna act like we're so concerned
For years holding a grudge
Instead of reaching out for a hug
Getting upset for no reason
No forgiving in any season
Over something that's minoot
Never wanted to settle your dispute
Now I'm a vapor's mist
Crying tears like I will be missed
But I'm gone and can't hear
So if you love me while I'm alive
make it loud and clear

written by Marvin Crutchfield aka Mr Poetry

WALK IN THE PARK

One day while I was walking in the park
I bumped into Yahuah
He said let me change your heart
I said as far as I know it's ok
I said maybe another day
Because I don't wanna waste your time
He said trust me and everything will be fine
You can do anything in my name
Just let me seal it on your brain
So we decided to take a seat
And He started to tell me about eternity
So I went under the knife
and accepted Yahuah offer of eternal life
So after my heart transplant
I began to feel like a brand new man
And that's all because of Yahuah the Savior
Who did me that special favor

written by Marvin Crutchfield aka Mr Poetry

W.A.R

In war there is no wrong or right
Just a terrible sight
Because they fight until no one's left
And all you see around you is death
It's the same old song told by the government
We're doing it to protect the innocent
Most of them are filled with debauchery
Because they don't care for you or me
All they do is exasperate other nations
But they don't realize we're all Yah's creation
Hopefully one day they'll understand
That it's not right to kill your fellow man
Because Yah says venges is mine's
but if they keep on
It's going to be the end of mankind

written by Marvin Crutchfield aka Mr Poetry

W.E.E.D

From every puff of weed
Don't you know that you're harming Yah's precious seed
In all that cloud of smoking
Your baby is coughing and choking
While you smoke to forget the past
Your baby is taking it in full blast
Don't you see my point
It's like handing your baby a joint
Please take heed
Don't harm Yah's precious seed

written by Marvin Crutchfield

WHO AM I

Since day one I've been very glad
To treat people of color very sad
If I murdered you like a dog
Or fed you slop from a hog
If I called you a nigger or boy
Or treated you like a broken toy
If I gave you a slave name
And continue to bring your people to shame
If all I do is lie
And don't care if your people die
If I'm making y'all feel inferior
While pretending that I'm superior
If I am a master thief
Stole everything and y'all a false belief
If I really hate myself
Because all I care about is wealth
If I broken people of color families apart
Because I have no heart
Who am I

written by Marvin Crutchfield aka Mr Poetry

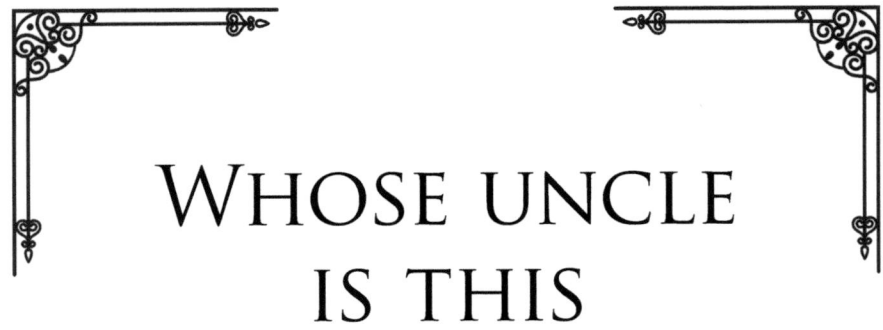

WHOSE UNCLE IS THIS

Whose uncle is this
Let us all reminisce
They call him uncle Sam
But in truth he never gave a damn
Look what he represents
The baphomet and dragon as the president
They worship false idols without a clue
And we fell for the same bullshit too
These idols are on everything we touch and see
And we did with glee
But my King Yah has opened my eyes
And He has shown me Babylon's demise
Yes these so called United States
Has sealed it's own fate
Look around and you see all these statues and false idols
That's why people are suicidal
America worships all the things made by man
And neglect King Yah who made them from the sand

written by Marvin Crutchfield aka Mr Poetry

WITHOUT NOTICE

You are some kind of worker
Being a professional twerker
All day long you shake that ass
Doing anything for that cash
You're young and pretty so you make a lot
Showing those thirstier than the desert men what you got
But time passes without notice
You're older now and you lost focus
Titties sag and your ass don't jiggle
You can't get on the pole
and slide down the middle
But to you it doesn't even feel strange
That you went from collecting paper bills
to spare change

written by Marvin Crutchfield aka Mr Poetry

WOE

All this time we were in church
Trying to get rid of our pain and hurt
The preacher with the laying of the hands
Thinking about his money in the grands
They hoop and holler
Put on a show for that all American dollar
But is no boundaries in greed
As they continue to plant their narcissistic seed
It's like their conscience is seared
Because they do this without fear
I mean scripture is holy and true
Yes King Yah is talking about me and you
No one will be exempt
So think about that time that you spent
Because Almighty Yah sits on His throne
And you will answer Him all alone
I guess some pastors ignore the word Woe (Jer 23)
If Yah says don't do it
Then the answer is no

written by Marvin Crutchfield aka Mr Poetry

YOU WOKE ME UP

Now that you woke up my other side
There is no place for you to hide
Because these words from me you can't maintain
I will leave you like a zombie with leaking brains
I watch as you're picking them up from the ground
Got you walking on eggshells without making a sound
Your mouth is fully agape
Because you just got tongue raped
You were left speechless
Yes I just exposed your weakness
So next time just leave me alone
Or you will be crying to your mama on the phone
Saying mom I can't take it no more
I'm tired of picking my mouth up from the floor
Cause Mr. Poetry always empties his chamber
Shoots me up with venom and anger

written by Marvin Crutchfield aka Mr Poetry

YOUR DOOR STEP

Just like China's Wahun
Or Vietnam's Saigon
It's nothing but plagues and pestilence
World War 3 is at our very essence
It's disguised under a different name
Where each country can point the blame
This Covid 19 is like an evil cloak
Suffocating you with a death choke
Flooding your ear gates with lies
To get you programmed and hypnotized
Now America believes the government's fables and stories
But won't tell them this Covid 19 was manufactured in a laboratory
They will go to great lengths to keep the truth from being revealed
So they can continue their mastery of murder, death and kill
But what happens when death comes to their door step
I guess they forgot about the boomerang effect

written by Marvin Crutchfield aka Mr, Poetry

www.ingramcontent.com/pod-product-compliance
Lightning Source LLC
Chambersburg PA
CBHW040846120626
46547CB00001B/55

9 781964 804316